ATYPICAL ANIMALS

This book was designed and produced by
Silver Goat Media, LLC. Fargo, ND U.S.A.
www.silvergoatmedia.com

ISBN-10: 1-944296-09-3
ISBN-13: 978-1-944296-09-4 (Silver Goat Media)

1.0 - 170317

A portion of the annual proceeds from the sale of this book are donated to the Longspur Prairie Fund.
www.longspurprairie.org

Dedicated to my nephew Michael.
Without him, this fuse would never have been lit.

And to my family and friends.
Their love and support made this entire journey
possible and worthwhile.

"In the depth of winter, I finally learned that within me there lay an invincible summer."
- Albert Camus

INTRODUCTION

Within these pages, you will find a collection of animals that are cute, cool, unusual, and unique. They create a vibrant ecosystem and help make our world a better and more fascinating place. Also, all these animals really exist.

For now, anyway.

It is an unfortunate truth that there are people who care more for themselves than the world around them. These people make the world an unhealthy place. And without a healthy world, vibrant ecosystems and the creatures who inhabit them cannot exist.

But you can help!

Work hard, care for others, and always choose knowledge and wisdom over pomp and charisma.

Do this and the world will be a far better and healthier place today, tomorrow, and in the future.

ATYPICAL ANIMALS

by Mark Elton

AXOLOTL

IF THE AXOLOTL LOSES AN ARM OR LEG, IT CAN GROW A NEW ONE.

BLUE FAIRY PENGUIN

THE BLUE FAIRY PENGUIN IS THE SMALLEST OF THE PENGUINS.

DUMBO OCTOPUS

THE DUMBO OCTOPUS IS NAMED BECAUSE OF ITS EAR-LIKE FINS THAT HELP IT MOVE THROUGH THE OCEAN.

ANGLERFISH

ONLY FEMALE ANGLERFISH HAVE A LURE OVER THEIR MOUTH.

FOSSA

THE FOSSA COMMUNICATES WITH OTHER FOSSA THROUGH BODY ODOR.

NARWHAL

SOMETIMES CALLED THE "UNICORN OF THE SEA," NARWHALS CAN HAVE 1, 2, OR NO TUSKS.

THORNY DRAGON

THORNY DRAGONS CHANGE COLOR BASED ON THE WEATHER.

PURPLE FROG

THE PURPLE FROG IS THE LAST OF A GROUP OF AMPHIBIANS WHICH EVOLVED 130 MILLION YEARS AGO.

JABIRU

THE JABIRU CAN INFLATE ITS NECK LIKE A BALLOON.

ISOPOD

ISOPODS LIVE IN A STATE OF SEMI-HIBERNATION, AND CAN GO YEARS WITHOUT EATING.

BLOBFISH

THE BLOBFISH IS OFTEN DESCRIBED AS THE UGLIEST ANIMAL IN THE WORLD.

ORCA

ORCAS SPEAK THEIR OWN LANGUAGE, CONSISTING OF CLICKS, WHISTLES, AND PULSES.

PALM CIVET

THE PALM CIVET LIVES ON A
DIET OF MANGOES AND COFFEE.

ORB WEAVER

FEMALE ORB WEAVERS ARE OVER TWICE AS LARGE AS THE MEN.

LOVEBIRD

LOVEBIRDS WILL MATE FOR LIFE AND PINE FOR ONE ANOTHER IF THEY GET SEPARATED.

YETI CRAB

YETI CRABS GROW THEIR OWN FOOD.

PANDA ANT

THE PANDA ANT IS ACTUALLY A TYPE OF WINGLESS WASP.

PINK FAIRY ARMADILLO

PINK FAIRY ARMADILLOS USE THEIR STRONG CLAWS TO SWIM THROUGH SAND.

WATER DEER

A NEWBORN WATER DEER IS SO SMALL, IT CAN FIT IN THE PALM OF YOUR HAND.

GREAT POTOO BIRD

THE GREAT POTOO BIRDS CAN SEE WITH THEIR EYES CLOSED.

There are so many more unique and unusual animals found across the world. Too many to fit in these pages.

Which unusual animals are your favorite?

What makes them special to you?

Visit **www.AtypicalAnimalBook.Club** and tell us.

The Atypical Animal Book Club has many more animals, facts, and fun activities for everyone!

Mark Elton is an artist, cartoonist, mythologist, game enthusiast, animator, amateur cryptographer, and adventurer. He graduated from Concordia College in 2007 with degrees in Studio Art and English Writing.

Mark finds inspiration in nature, humanity, and technology; his art explores the connections, juxtapositions, and overlaps between the three. Mark's work has been displayed in galleries across North America.

You can learn more about Mark and his projects at www.BiblioTrek.com.

Made in the USA
Lexington, KY
14 June 2018